To Debbie & Al   02/03

KEY WEST COLOR

Look for the beauty
in life . . .
It is within you
Always
Alan S. Maltz

KEY WEST COLOR

ALAN S. MALTZ

INTRODUCTION BY GEORGE MURPHY

Light
Flight
Publications

KEY WEST, FLORIDA

For Aunt May… Your unconditional love and faith are the source of my strength and inspiration.

FIRST EDITION
4th printing

Publisher's Cataloging in Publication

Maltz, Alan S.
    Key West Color / Alan S. Maltz; introduction by George Murphy.
    p. cm.
    Preassigned LCCN: 94-076915.
    ISBN 0-9626677-2-2

    1. Key West (Fla.)--Pictorial works.   I. Title.
F319.K4M37 1995   917.59'41
                               QBI94-1327

All inquiries regarding the works of Alan S. Maltz, including the images in this book, may be directed to the publisher.

Published by Light Flight Publications
1210 Duval Street
Key West, Florida 33040
Studio
Tel (305) 294-0005 Fax (305) 294-0097
Office
Tel (305) 745-2832 Fax (305) 745-8809
www.alanmaltz.com
email:visions@alanmaltz.com

Printed in Hong Kong

"…time past …has a lovely way of remaining time present in Key West."

Tennessee Williams

Key West is probably the best-known small town on the planet. Though tiny enough, it is rumored, to fit into New York's Central Park, Key West has managed - through its rich history, its remote location, and its ravishing natural beauty - to earn a notation in every national and international map. The island city has created its own legend and does indeed fly its own banner as well: a queen Conch standing proudly against a golden-bladed sun in a field of blue. Also known as the Conch Republic - fiercely independent, proudly tolerant, and aggressively generous - Key West is home to a permanent population of about 30,000 souls.

"Home is where the heart is," and no true romantic's heart does not have "Key West" etched somewhere on its walls. Few have visited without taking home the images of its turquoise waters, its starry nights, its rustling palms, and its flourishes of gingerbread and bougainvillea. Local legend has it that, if you get sand in your shoes while visiting, you will return one day.

This mere six square miles of limestone rock is dotted with over fifty bars, scores of great restaurants, and a hundred or so hotels and guest houses, serving host to over 1.2 million visitors per year. Key West sits like a jewel in the middle of the sea, just off the coast of America. Its air quality is second to no other city. The average annual temperature of 77° rarely varies more than 10° in either direction, with a record low of 41° and a record high of 97°. It has never seen frost or snow. Perennially sunny, the island averages only 39 inches of rain per year.

Renowned for its frost-free climate, azure waters, tropical flora and fauna, sport fishing, its easy pace and laissez-faire tolerance of alternative lifestyles, Key West continues to draw a new and novel mix of drop-outs and developers, expatriates and idealists, writers and romantics, runaways and roustabouts of all persuasions. Visitors frequently note the warmth and friendliness of its inhabitants. Asking someone for directions may lead to a good recommendation for lunch.

Key West can boast of the most unusual and eclectic population of any American city. "Key West isn't Florida," says a young boy in Joy Williams' short story, "The Blue Men." And it's true. With its cosmopolitan and well-educated population, it's something of a cultural Noah's Ark adrift in the Gulf of Mexico - sending out white doves which always seem to loop back and nest in the branches of its own sturdy banyan trees. Visitors always seem amazed at how many Key Westers they encounter who inform them, "I came down for a weekend six years ago ... and I'm still here." Something indefinable - a balance of exotic remoteness, cultural marginality, and artistic intellect - beckons many to Key West, where, until recently, the *Sunday New York Times* often arrived on Monday and local phone numbers contained only five digits.

Though life on the island seems less marginal and remote each year, people in the Keys live not just at the edge of America but also

on the edge of danger where the next hurricane could, in the words of novelist Thomas Sanchez, "wipe the slate clean." Though Key West has not taken a direct hit from a hurricane since 1919, Solares Hill, the highest point of land on the island, is only 15 feet above sea level. A Force 5 hurricane with a 20-foot "storm surge" could easily erase the island. Obviously, the risk, for many, is outweighed by the privilege of living in paradise.

The native population, those born on the island, refer to themselves as "Conchs," and represent a unique mix of Bahamian, Cuban, and New England seafaring heritage. Many well-known Conch families have been here for seven or more generations. Some confess to having never been off the island.

It has also attracted generations of artists and writers who popularized the mythology of the island. Key West has been home to Ernest Hemingway, Tennessee Williams, Elizabeth Bishop, John Ciardi, John Hersey, Richard Wilbur, Philip Caputo, Alison Lurie, James Merrill, and Thomas McGuane, among many others. More Pulitzer Prize winners have lived in Key West per capita than in any other city.

Island mythology also crosses into popular culture. Novels, movies, and television programs set in Key West have introduced many to the island indirectly. Pop star Jimmy Buffett's lament of being "Wasted away again in Margaritaville," has become a landmark goal of many visitors.

Key West is also known for its sizable, accepted, and openly gay population which has contributed greatly to the island's burgeoning tourism and business community.

There's no up-town or down-town in Key West, no dress codes even for the finest of restaurants. Tolerance is the rule and differences are to be celebrated. Even daily life in Key West includes a certain off-beat sense of celebration. Each day's setting sun is celebrated and sometimes even applauded at Mallory Square, while artisans, musicians, and street performers pack the city pier with visitors as the famed and often glorious Key West sunsets shimmer over the Gulf of Mexico. During October's Fantasy Fest each year, the city is as alive as New Orleans during Mardi Gras. The streets swell with revelers for a festive week of international and local costume contests, street fairs, and parades.

Despite its reputation for being "laid-back," Key Westers are hard-working people. They have to be. Virtually everything on the island has to be imported on a one-way truck. Add to that the desirability of island property and it is easy to understand why the cost of living is the highest in the state. With tourism as its only true economic base, and relatively low-paying tourism – related jobs as the most common denominator, it is clear why many members of the working population hold two – or more – jobs in order to live in, what they consider, paradise.

Although Key West is, in fact, the westernmost of the Florida Keys, its name was corrupted from the Spanish Cayo Hueso or "Island of Bones," dubbed such when Spanish explorers set foot on a landscape littered with the human bones of Calusa Indians and unfortunate seafarers. Of late, it has also been nicknamed "The Conch Republic" and "Margaritaville," (as much a state of mind as it is a comment on one of the daily rituals).

Key West is in fact the "end of the road," Mile "Zero" of the original U.S. East Coast Route 1, which stretches to the town of Fort Kent, Maine. As the demarcation sign on Whitehead Street would suggest it is, to some, the "end of the rainbow" as well. For others, it is the end of the line, as far as they can run, the tip of the American funnel, spilling into the nation's most interesting mixing-pot, in which the resulting cultural gumbo may either be delicately sipped or tossed down with reckless abandon.

How is it that this tiny American island community has achieved the visibility and some of the romance and intrigue of cities like Tangiers, Havana, Majorca, or Rio? Myth is a powerful force and it is woven like a tapestry with the rich history of Key West.

Thousands of years ago the seas receded, exposing the coral and limestone reef tracts which would become the Florida Keys. Modern recorded history of the Keys begins with Ponce de Leon's 1513 discovery of the islands he named *Los Martires*, the martyrs –

after the twisted, tortured appearance of the dense and tangled native mangrove trees. Indian pottery and artifacts, however, have been excavated which date back to 1200 B.C. The effects of numerous tribes have been found, but it was largely the Calusa tribe that inhabited the Keys until the 1760's, when invading mainland tribes drove them southward, island by island, until they were massacred on Key West.

With its deep water port at the juncture of two oceans and its sub-tropical climate, Key West had long been a haven for pirates and for Spanish adventurers. Within months after the first settlement was established in 1822, the U.S. Navy sent the tyrannical Commodore David Porter, a veteran of the Barbary Coast pirate wars, to Key West. Porter launched a bloody and successful campaign to rid the Caribbean of piracy. Soon after, the previously risky business of shipping through the Florida Straits thrived. So, too, did the practice of wrecking, the salvaging of valuable cargo from the innumerable ships which ventured too close to the unmarked shallows and reefs off the coast of the Keys.

In 1825 Congress enacted legislation which required that all salvaged goods taken from wrecks be brought to a U.S. port for arbitration. For the entire Caribbean Basin, that port was Key West. Soon after, as auction houses were built on the waterfront to sell the salvaged spoils from some of the richest cargoes ever lost at sea, Key West became the wealthiest city per capita in America.

By 1831 industry had arrived: ship-fitting, turtling, salt manufacturing, and cigar-making. One cigar factory alone employed 50 workers. Late in the next decade, it was discovered that the high-quality sea sponges used so commonly among the local population could fetch a substantial price in the North. Another industry was begun and Bahamian "spongers" arrived in droves. By 1850, a hospital, a school, and several churches had been built and a quarter of the island had been cleared for settlement. New England and Bahamian seamen, fortune-seekers, buyers, adjusters, shipwrecked merchant sailors, and Cubans were the foundation of the ever-expanding ethnic and cultural mix of this increasingly cosmopolitan island city.

In 1845 the War Department began construction of Fort Zachary Taylor, which would later serve as headquarters for the successful naval blockade of the Confederacy. During the Civil War, as many as 299 ships would be anchored at one time in the harbor at Key West, the only Union-held city south of the Mason-Dixon Line.

After the war, the newly-constructed navigational lighthouses led to the decline of the wrecking industry, but the Cuban cigar-making industry grew phenomenally. The subsequent immigration of thousands of Cubans during the Ten Years War in Cuba made Key West the cigar capital of the world and a haven for Cuban revolutionaries.

Although the Florida Keys are commonly perceived as an exotic island outgrowth of Miami, it is, ironically, Miami which grew from the Keys. Five years before the U.S. Navy first ventured, in 1835, into the wilderness at the mouth of the Miami River to establish Fort Dallas, the city of Key West had already been chartered and surveyed. Fifty years before Miami expanded beyond a settlement of mere shacks and tents, Key West had become more populous than all the rest of Florida. In fact, Miami's most noted pioneer, Mrs. Julia Tuttle, credited with having brought the Flagler railroad to Miami, arrived by sailboat to Biscayne Bay in November, 1891 – from Key West.

The Cuban San Carlos Institute and Opera House, opened in 1871, made Key West a culturally vital city. On its stage, the Cuban leader Jose Marti spoke and the legendary Pavlova danced.

Fire destroyed fifty acres of downtown city property in 1886 but by the following year, steamship service was established between Tampa, Key West, and Havana, and reconstruction of the city was vigorously underway. By 1889 there was an electric lighting plant; by 1890, a turtle-canning factory and an ice-house.

As the city of Miami was being established, the city of Key West was again undergoing drastic change. At the turn of the century, Jose Marti's Cuban Revolutionary Party was running guns and men to Cuba. Then, with the explosion of the USS Maine in Havana Harbor in 1898, the island became the pivotal military installation of the Spanish-American War.

The staggering and unflaggable vision of Henry Flagler finally

connected the island of Key West to the continent. In 1905 Flagler began work on one of the most monumental construction feats in American history - the "Railroad That Went To Sea" - extending his tracks over 150 miles of water and islands. When the project was completed in 1912, Key West became and stayed the "Gateway to Cuba"; steamers, ferries, and cargo ships filled the harbor.

One can easily imagine the island of Key West in those days as being caught up in a dream of future success and luxury. A disastrous succession of events, however, soon were to drag Key West down an economic black hole.

First, labor problems and destructive hurricanes led to the migration of the cigar industry to the Tampa area. Next, an underwater blight destroyed the sponge beds, and the island's second industry died. The Florida land boom collapsed in the mid-20's and those few tourists who did arrive were, more often than not, just passing through to Cuba. Then came The Great Depression, with fewer and fewer trains arriving in town. In 1934, 80% of the population was on relief and there was even talk of abandoning the island and resettling its population. Key West, once the wealthiest city per capita in America, was now the poorest.

Then came the final blow. On Labor Day of 1935, the strongest hurricane in recorded history hit the upper Florida Keys. Winds of over 200 miles an hour and storm surge "tidal waves" killed hundreds and tumbled the railroad into the ocean.

Into this scenario stepped the handsome, eccentric, and inventive Julius Stone, director of the Florida Federal Emergency Relief Agency (FERA) and, some say, the conceptual architect of the Key West we know today. A master of publicity, Stone's response to the economic decay was to issue a "Surrender of Key West," which made national headlines. He dressed in Bermuda shorts (unheard of at the time and referred to by locals as "underwear") and organized a city-wide cleaning and coconut palm planting effort, then traveled the country proclaiming Key West as America's new tropical island paradise.

In 1938 the Overseas Highway and world-famous Seven-Mile Bridge replaced the railroad while airline service was becoming popular. Stone's vision materialized as tourists flocked to the island.

It was during the 30's as well that the seeds of Key West's reputation as a haven for writers and artists were sown. Renowned writers such as Robert Frost, Wallace Stevens, and John Dos Passos, among others, were regular visitors; Ernest Hemingway and, later, Tennessee Williams made the island their home.

After World War II, when the military expanded control from 50 to nearly 3,000 acres in the lower Keys and made Key West a major convoy center, the island settled into a period of reconstruction and readjustment, focusing again on tourism—no doubt aided by President Harry S. Truman's choice of Key West for his "Little White House" retreat.

In the '60's and '70's, smuggling was a major industry in the Keys and the somewhat secret fortunes of many of the city's most successful businessmen were made as bales of marijuana were openly unloaded on the city docks.

In 1982, two years after the Mariel Boatlift, the U.S. Border Patrol, searching for illegal aliens and smuggled drugs, set up a roadblock on Highway 1 which backed up traffic to and from the Keys for hours. In an echo of Julius Stone's publicity of the 30's, the city fathers, reacting to the imminent financial disaster of a tourist economy, seceded from the Union, establishing the Conch Republic. They fired one shot, surrendered, and applied for foreign aid. The publicity stunt succeeded in removing the roadblocks and making worldwide headlines. The celebration of the event in April is, to this day, a city tradition.

Over the past decade Key West has changed, as author Tom McGuane once observed, "stroboscopically." Riding the crest of a surging wave of tourism, its only true industry, the number of hotel rooms on the island has tripled. In the face of such success, the city now faces the challenge of protecting their most vital resources – one of the largest historic districts in the United States and the only living coral reef in North America.

Key West is a city which celebrates itself, its history, its diversity and its various reputations in many ways. Festivals and parties punctuate the tourist season. The social calendar – fishing tournaments and art festivals, literary seminars and world premiere plays, house and garden tours, international power boat and yacht races, and a lighted boat parade – goes on 365 days a year. Most notable perhaps is Fantasy Fest, Key West's answer to Mardi Gras. Visitors from around the world descend on a ten-day event in October that culminates with a parade through Old Town that draws an estimated 50,000 celebrants.

Key West is for many the greatest city in America. Its population is a patchwork quilt of the most culturally diverse elements imaginable, stitched together with the sturdy threads of acceptance and the desire to celebrate life.

Over seventy years ago, Florida historian Jefferson Browne wrote of Key West,

> …when the day is done, he [the sun] sinks back into the western deep, attended by a pageantry of color that can be produced only by the Master Artist; streaks of red across cerulean blue, fade to delicate pinks and greens and soft tones of gray, whilst the sun from his place below the horizon send his rays through the clouds, till they resemble mountains of molten gold.
>
> Come weal, come woe; come progress, come decay; come nature with her beauty, come man with his mistakes; nothing can mar the sky, the water, the sunrise and sunset, which make the unchanging and unchangeable Key West!

Approaching Key West   *Overseas Highway*

Aerial Highlights   *Gulf of Mexico*

Islands Overview   *Gulf of Mexico*

Orchids / Brassavola Nodosa

Great White Heron

Sunset over Gulf

Flats Fishing at Dusk

Alternative Lifestyle *Houseboat Row*

The Ultimate Conch Cruiser   *AIA*

Haitian Art

Street Artist *Front Street*

Giving and Receiving *Thomas Street*

First Communion

Vanishing Point *Smathers Beach*

Sunset Medley

Late Afternoon *Caroline Street*

Pineapple Fence   *Caroline Street*

Tropical Perspective *Duval Street*

Gingerbread *Southard Street*

Creative Costume *Fantasy Fest*

Curious Encounter *Fantasy Fest*

Oil Drilling Protest *Stock Island*

Osprey and Liberty *Oversaes Highway*

Roseate Spoonbills at Dawn

Roseate Spoonbills *Overseas Highway*

Buoy House *Angela Street*

Houseboat *Houseboat Row*

Interlocking Palms

Nature Bike Tour Guide   *Galveston Lane*

Christmas Cycle *Eaton Street*   Dolphin House *Fleming Street*

Christmas Dressing   *William Street*

Ray Charles at The Reach

One Man Band at Mallory Square

St. Paul's Episcopal Church *Duval Street*

Moonrise Over St. Mary's   *Truman Avenue*

Old Friends *Simonton Street*

Key West Humor

Old Boca Chica Lounge *Stock Island*

Heartbreak Hotel *Duval Street*

Laughing Gulls

Bottlenose Dolphins

Classic Gingerbread *Eaton Sreet*

Old Cuban Consulate *Eaton Street*

Mangrove Silhouette *Overseas Highway*

Royal Poinciana *Southard Street*

Self Promoter   *Duval Street*

Ted *Eaton Street*

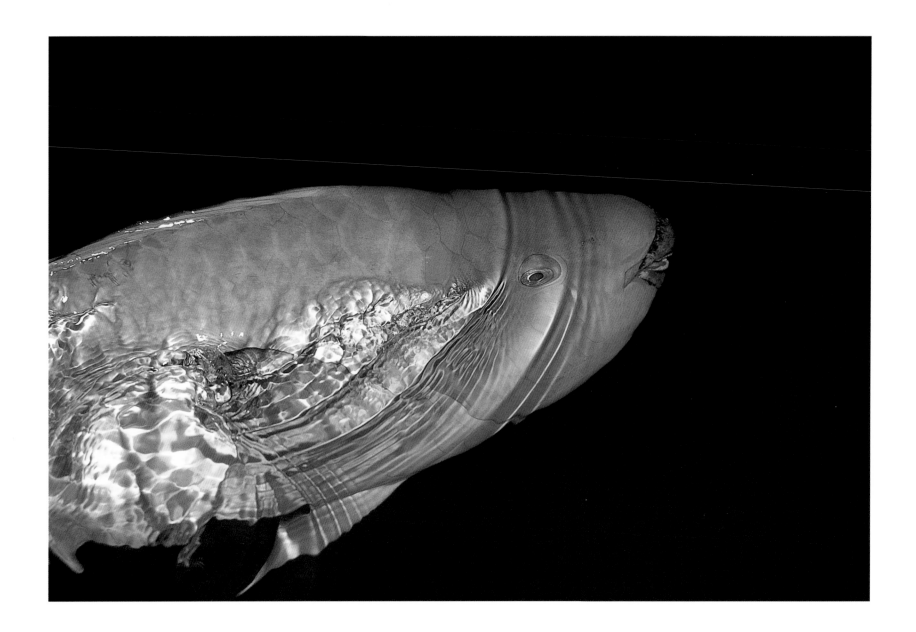

Parrotfish

Mermaid Down Duval *Fantasy Fest*

Whaling Research Vessel

Osprey and Nest *Overseas Highway*

Hemingway House *Whitehead Street*

Hemingway Typewriter

Artist Teresa Willis

Hemingway Look-alike Contest   *Duval Street*

Old Custom House *Front Street*

Architectural Detail / Old Custom House

Anvil Cloud with Lightning *Overseas Highway*

Funnel Cloud   *Overseas Highway*

Vertigo Man *Fantasy Fest*

  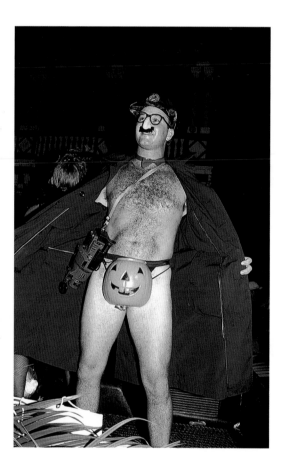

Fantasy Fest Follies

620 Southard Street

Classic Key West Architecture

Macaws

Tropical Relations

Old Coast Guard Building   *Front Street*

Key West Lighthouse *Whitehead Street*

Strand *Duval Street*   Little White House *Truman Annex*

Southernmost House *Duval Street*   Audubon House *Whitehead Street*

Captain Frank

Mirror Image *Overseas Highway*

Abstract by Design *Smathers Beach*

Patterns *Smathers Beach*

Literal Group *Fantasy Fest*

Ladies in Waiting *Fantasy Fest*

Daybreak *Overseas Highway*

Mangrove Sunset   *Overseas Highway*

Parky   Pritam   Joe

Roy

Feather Man

Love 22

Palms and Shadows *Truman Annex*

Sunset Silhouette *Overseas Highway*

Dominique and His Flying House Cats

Dominique / Sunset Celebration *Mallory Square*

Captain Bucky

Spirit of the Conch Republic   *White Street*

Islands Sunset *Overseas Highway*

Frank Simon / Sunset Performer *Mallory Square*

Manatee

Manatee Houseboat *Lazy Way Lane*

Snoopy   *Marvin Key*

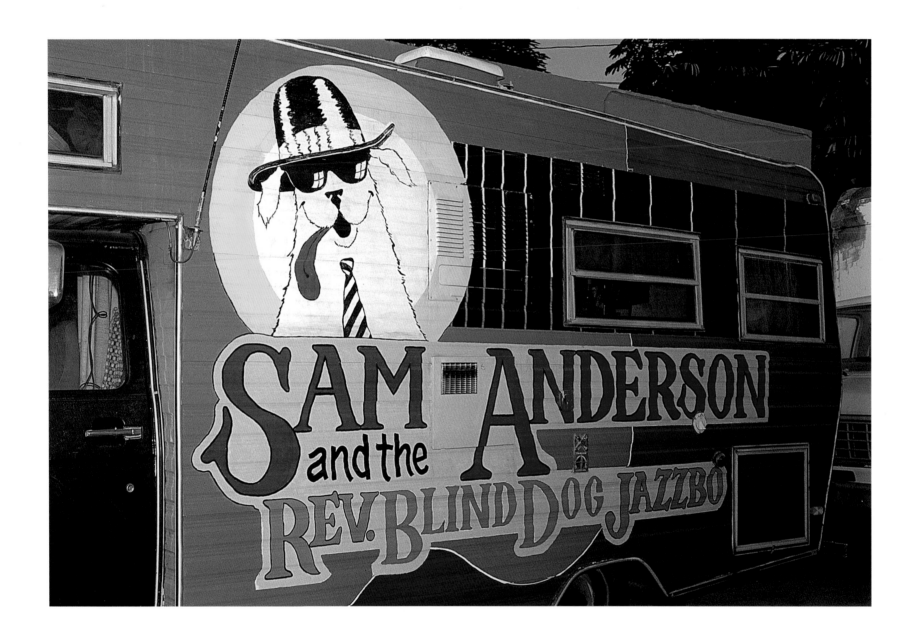

Unmistakably Key West *Virginia Street*

Seahorse Doors   *Truman Avenue*

Steppin' Out / Queen Conch

Caribbean Style / Fantasy Fest

Fantasy Feast

Lloyd

Author John Cole

Mr. & Mrs. Claus *Harris Avenue*

Housegift   *Houseboat Row*

Mallory Sunset

Mallory Pier at Sunset

Submerged Vessel   *Key West Harbor*   Casting Director   *A1A*

Early Morning *Smathers Beach*

Cuban Rafters Rescued

Freedom *U.S. Coast Guard Station Key West*

Bald Eagle Over Boca Chica

Trinity Presbyterian Church *Simonton Street*

Funeral Parade *Thomas Street*

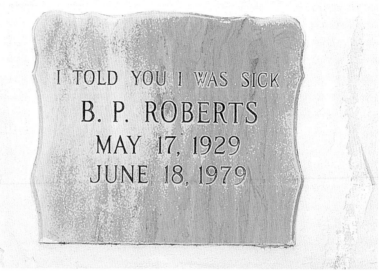

Key West Cemetery

Car with Character   *Greene Street*

Captain Tony

Will Soto Walking Tightrope *Mallory Square*

Will Soto / Sunset Performer *Mallory Square*

Local Resident

Mallory Performer

Leonard Bernstein

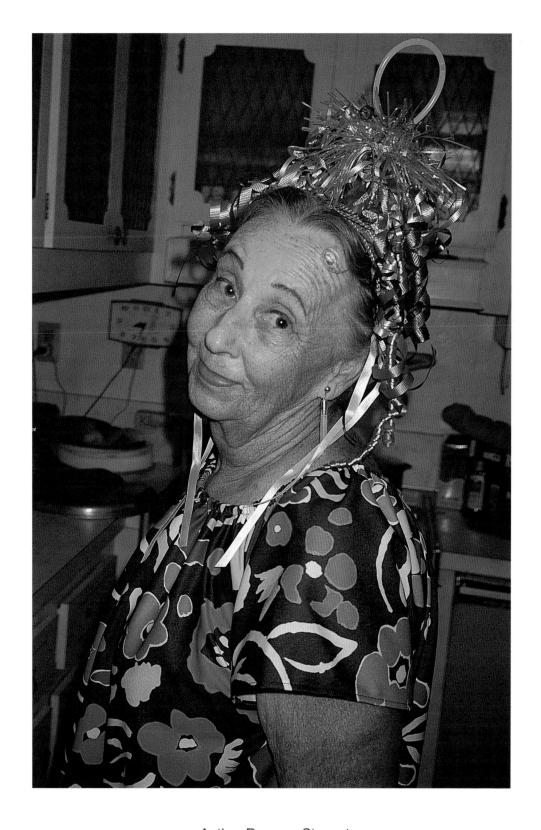

Author Ramona Stewart

Watercolors *Smathers Beach*

Weather in Transition *Overseas Highway*

Artist's Palette and Brushes

Nature's Palette *Key Haven*

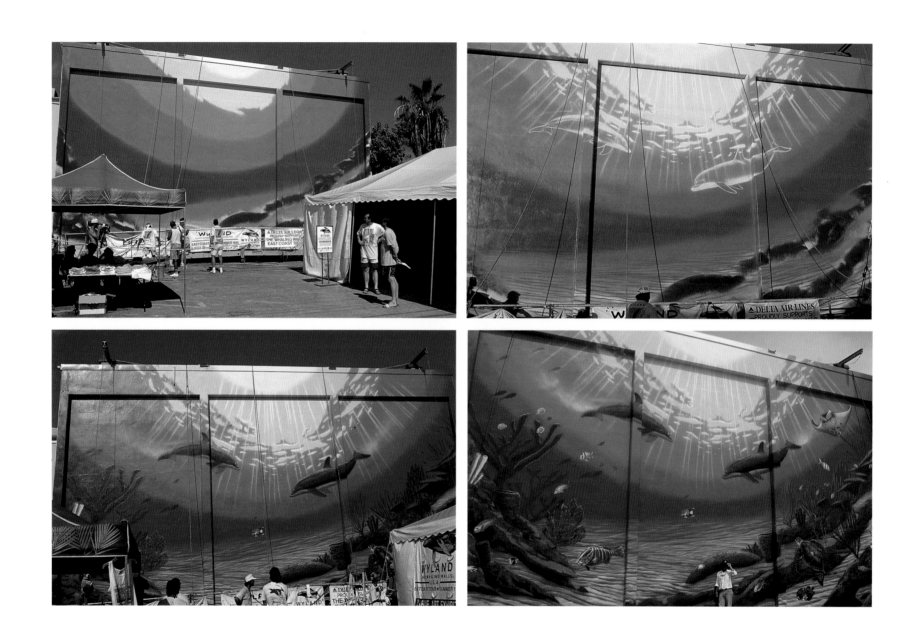

4 Stages of Wyland's Whaling Wall #52   *William Street*

Wyland / Environmental Marine Life Artist

Cuban Tree Frog Atlantic Green Turtle

Lower Keys Marsh Rabbit

Burrowing Owls

Goombay Festival   *Bahama Village*

Mother and Child / Goombay Festival

Key West Tradition *Stock Island*

Noah Coakley Allen

Outnumbered *Lands End Village*

Attack Kitten

Naturally Acting

Acting Naturally

Flower Power *Eaton Street*

Key West Sharkatecture *Elizabeth Street*

Keeper of the Nest / Osprey

Homecomings / Osprey

October Thirty-First

Catwitch of Key West

Out on the Town *Duval Street*

Self Expression *Duval Street*

Viewpoint *Smathers Beach*

After Hours *Smathers Beach*

On The Beach

Day's End   *Smathers Beach*

Yacht Race

Father & Son

Brown Pelican *Overseas Highway*

Greenpeace at Sunset *Truman Annex Pier*

Jimmy Buffett and Cheeseburger *Salt Ponds*

Sign with Personality   *Lands End Village*

Yacht Race Crew

Offshore Action / Yacht Race

Sunset Show *Truman Annex Pier*

Southernmost Serenade / Southernmost Point *Whitehead Street*

Carefree Days

Catch of the Day

Different Strokes

Recycled Junk Raft / Earth Day *Fort Taylor Beach*

Conch House   *Southard Street*

Character Study   Ashe Street

Royal Poinciana *Casa Marina Court*

Wilhelmina Harvey / Mayor Emeritus & County Commissioner

Classic Wood Structures

Phillip Burton House with Phillip Burton *Angela Street*

Dramatic Endings

Tapestry by Nature

Last Flight to Paradise / Great White Heron

The End

KEY WEST WILDLIFE

Key West and the Florida Keys are one of the most unique and biologically diverse regions in the world. Some varieties of flora and fauna native to the area exist nowhere else on earth. A prime example is the newly discovered and endangered "Lower Keys Marsh Rabbit", (page 141).

The existence of many of these species are now threatened due to human overpopulation, destruction of natural habitat and pollution. Some are already extinct. The problem is not just local; it is global. The following paragraph, taken from *Celebrities of Nature - Endangered and Selected Species of Florida*, addresses this issue.

"The balance of nature is delicate and complex. Tipping the scales in either direction can be catastrophic. Never, in the history of the world, has one dominant species (mankind) so deliberately altered the natural forces of our planet. Global warming, holes in the ozone, air and water pollution, destruction of the rainforests, diseased coral reefs and vanishing wildlife are all evidence that humankind is not working in harmony with nature. We are just beginning to understand how plants, animals and elements are all related to each other, and us to them. Their health and balance is our health and survival."

We must do the little things that add up to make a difference. A greater respect for the earth must emerge. Most of all, a new consciousness must evolve that will put living things ahead of economic gain.

Alan S. Maltz

REFERENCES

PAGES 2, 42, 43
ROSEATE SPOONBILL *(Ajaia ajaja)* **STATUS:** Species of Special Concern. From the 1850's to the early 1900's, plume hunters slaughtered thousands of Spoonbills for their plumage, nearly wiping out the entire population. Today, the Spoonbill is protected, but human encroachment and development still pose great threats. **DATA:** 30-32" in length, 53" wingspan, pink with white necks and backs and a very flat spoon-shaped bill. **HABITAT:** Mangroves and salt ponds. **DIET:** Shrimp and fish. **REMARKS:** One of Florida's most colorful birds, often mistaken for Flamingos which are much taller and have angled beaks. Spoonbill now protected by law, but additional aquisitions of Spoonbill habitats as preserves are needed to ensure stability of the species.

PAGES 23, 184
GREAT WHITE HERON *(Ardea henodias occidentalis)* **STATUS:** Not listed by state, but is listed in Rare & Endangered Biota of Florida as a species of special concern. Birds suffered severe decline by the 1930's, hunted for food, as well as the Great Hurricane of 1935 (and Hurricane Donna in 1960). Today, quality of habitat in Florida Bay is on the decline, with less fish and less fresh water. **DATA:** Largest of all American Herons, white with yellow bill and legs (Great Egret has black legs), 50" in length, 70" wingspan. **DIET:** Fish and frogs. **HABITAT:** Shallow bays and mangrove islands in the Florida Keys. **REMARKS:** Formation of the Great White Heron National Wildlife Refuge in the 1930's and the Key West Wildlife Refuge provide birds with needed protection. The Great White Heron is a color morph of the Great Blue Heron, and it is no longer considered a separate species. This phase only occurs in Florida and the Caribbean.

PAGES 41, 69, 152, 153
OSPREY *(Pandion haliaetus)* **STATUS:** Species of special concern (Monroe County), suffered decline due to pesticides in the food chain. Toxic chemicals affect calcium metabolism, resulting in thin-shelled and often infertile eggs, similar to the eagle and other "Raptors." **DATA:** Bird of prey, (frequently mistaken for the Bald Eagle), 21-24" in length, 54-72" wingspan, with a dark band across its face and white breast. (The Bald Eagle has a dark breast). Commonly called "Sea Eagle", fish comprise its entire diet . . . flies over prey, hovers and plunges feet-first to extract the fish, using sharp spring-like projectors on the bottom of its feet to help grip slippery catches. Frequently builds nests on top of telephone poles, expanding and improving the nests from year to year. **REMARKS:** Banning DDT and other pesticides in 1972 helped the osprey make a recovery. Stricter government regulations and testing policies of potentially devastating chemicals must continue.

PAGE 58
LAUGHING GULL *(Larus articilla)* **STATUS:** Not listed but numbers have declined in recent years, possibly due to destruction of coastal marshes and other suitable nesting sites. **DATA:** 15-17" in length. In summer, adults head turns black (black hood) and back to white in winter. Young birds are dark brown with white rump. Mature birds are white with gray wings and black wing tips. **DIET:** Feed by grabbing tiny fish from water while in flight but do not dive into water like terns. Occasional uninvited guests at seaside picnics. Breeds along coast from Maine to Florida and Gulf of Mexico. Winters from Virginia south. **REMARKS:** Commonly called "Sea Gull" although scientifically no such species exists. Opens stubborn shellfish by carrying them to great heights, then dropping them on hard surfaces. Continued development of salt marsh areas will lead to further decline of the species.

PAGE 59
BOTTLENOSE DOLPHIN *(Tursiops truncatus)* **STATUS:** Not listed, but in the last few years there have been several heavy, unexplained die-offs, resulting in hundreds of dolphins washing ashore for no apparent reason. The cause could be viral or by toxic waste/pollution in the ocean ecosystem. **DATA:** 3-13' in length, generally dark gray, but individuals may vary from albino white to nearly black. The "nose" is well-defined but short. **DIET:** Wide variety of fish, squid, shrimp and crabs. Observed following boats, eating fish scraps thrown overboard. They locate their food by using "echo-location" (projecting sound waves and listening for the echo). **REMARKS:** Also known as the Bottlenose Porpoise, dolphins are intelligent, trainable, lovable and gentle. Wild dolphins will approach humans, close enough to be touched, sadly their lifespan in captivity is shortened considerably. They can communicate between themselves, but communication with humans is still a goal. Dolphins are now participating in promising research with autistic children and cancer patients. The (Florida Keys) Dolphin Research Center is helping bridge the gap between dolphins and humans.

PAGE 66
PARROTFISH *(Papegaaivisse)* **STATUS:** Parrotfish are not listed, but their habitat is in trouble. Seagrass die-offs and the decline in the quality of our coral reefs pose a threat to these and many other unique marine species. **DATA:** Named for the their beak-like jaw and brilliant color. Mainly herbivorous. Few of the larger species feed in part on live coral. Found on coral reefs, along rocky shores and in seagrass beds. Unusual sexual development starts as drably-colored females (primary phase) turn into vibrant-colored males (terminal stage). 14 known species in North American. **REMARKS:** Our only living reef in North America is being destroyed. Greatest single threat: people, physical damage from careless boaters (anchoring on, touching, standing on or harvesting live coral). Land-based pollution: nutrient loading (septic tank leakage, fertilizers, pesticides) cause "blackband disease" and algal growth. Marine debris kills or injures many birds and marine species. In Key West, Reef Relief organized to preserve and protect this unique and fragile ecosystem.

PAGES 82, 83
PARROT *(Psittaciformes)* **STATUS:** Not listed, only native (Florida) parrot, the Carolina Parakeet, is now extinct. Habitat destruction (disappearing rainforests) and the pet trade have brought some varieties of parrots to the point of extinction. **DATA:** Native to tropical and moderate zones in Central and South America, Africa, Austrailia, Asia, New Zealand and New Guinea. Smallest parrot: Pygmy (4"), largest: Hyacinth Macaws (40"). **DIET:** Seeds, nuts and fruits. Travels in noisy flocks, only mimics in captivity. Lay 1-10 perfectly round eggs, both parents partake in nesting duties, lifespan (small species) 8-20 years, (largest) 40-65 years. Intelligent and easily trained. **REMARKS:** Parrots are part of Key West lifestyle. Some, escaped from captivity are living in the wild in Florida. Deforestation not only threatens wildlife, but unbalances natural systems and is partially responsible for global warming. The pet trade has pillaged rainforests and jungles of many exotic species. Many are now extinct or rare. International "Red List" prohibits trading threatened birds (approximately 1,000,000 birds captured annually, with at least a 50% mortality rate due to capture or horrific transport conditions).

PAGE 106
FLORIDA MANATEE *(Trichechus manatus)* **STATUS:** Endangered, less than 1500 remain in the wild. By the turn of the century, hunted almost to extinction for hides, blubber, meat and oil. Today, habitat destruction, boating accidents, canal locks, fishing lines, disease, cold water and human contact all contribute to injury and worse. **DATA:** Aquatic torpedo-shaped mammal, paddle-like tail, 8-15' in length, weight approximately one ton. Very gentle and passive, strict vegetarian, eats 60-100 pounds of aquatic vegetation daily, helps keep waterways free flowing and clean. Has 50-year lifespan, is partially nocturnal, and must surface for air every few minutes even while asleep. **PREDATORS:** Sharks, alligators, crocodiles and humans. Highly evolved, with close ties to the elephant family. Mermaid myths said to originate from manatee relative, the "Dugong". **REMARKS:** Florida Manatee Sanctuary Act of 1978 established a refuge for manatees. Safe boating practices near manatee areas, minimizing human contact and public awareness can save lives. "Save the Manatee Club", in Maitland, Florida, organized to help manatees.

PAGE 111
QUEEN CONCH *(Strombus gigas)* **STATUS:** Not listed, exploited species, season is closed due to overharvesting. DATA: 8-10" in length, the second largest species of Strombus Conch, with a rich pinkish interior and white exterior. Large snail-like creature inside never leaves the shell, just stretches its head and "foot" out to feed or move. A secretion by the animal's living tissue produces the non-living shell. Main component of the shell is calcium carbonate (the same substance found in our teeth and bones). Approximately 1 out of every 10,000 contain a valuable "Conch Pearl". **DIET:** Wide variety of marine plants and scavenged organic mater. It is found in a wide range of underwater environments, from shallow, clear water to depths of nearly 500 feet. **REMARKS:** The Conch is the symbol of Key West (and the Florida Keys). The ornamental shell and the conch meat are both popular, which resulted in overfishing. Under state protection, conch served in Florida restaurants are from the Caribbean.

PAGE 124
AMERICAN BALD EAGLE *(Haliaeetus leucocephalus)* **STATUS:** Threatened in Florida, threatened federally. Near extinction during 1960's because of pesticides in food chain (fish). Toxic chemicals, when absorbed, affect calcium metabolism, resulting in thin-shelled and often infertile eggs. Adults outnumber young. Alteration of habitat and shooting also decrease numbers. Of the 1,000 Southern Bald Eagles remaining, 700 are in Florida with seven nesting pair in the Keys. DATA: Large bird of prey, 30-31" length, 72-90" wingspan, two subspecies; Northern (slightly larger) and Southern (Florida has the most breeding pairs). **DIET:** Fish and waterfowl. Performs spectacular courtship ritual known as "cartwheels display," national bird since 1782, (Ben Franklin opposed making Bald Eagle the official symbol . . . his choice was the Wild Turkey). **REMARKS:** Rare success! Eagle made sufficient enough recovery to have federal status changed form Endangered to Threatened. Banning DDT and similar pesticides in 1972 helped the eagle and other "Raptors" make a comeback. Stricter government regulations and testing policies for potentially hazardous chemicals may have reduced this situation.

PAGE 140A
CUBAN TREE FROG *(Osteopilus hyla septentrionalis)* **STATUS:** Not listed. Transplanted Tree Frog population is currently stable. **DATA:** 1.5 - 5.5" in length, largest Tree Frog in North America. Warty skin (green, bronze or gray), enormous toe pads, skin on top of head is fused to the skull. **HABITAT:** moist and shady places in trees and shrubs or around houses. Species probably introduced by accident into Key West in vegetable produce brought from Cuba around 1900, then spread to the mainland. Nocturnal, eats anything it can catch and swallow; insects, spiders and other frogs. **REMARKS:** Very adaptable to many habitats. Author was rudely awakened by this very frog jumping on his face in the middle of the night, then quickly proceeded to negotiate a contract to appear in this book.

PAGE 140B
ATLANTIC GREEN TURTLE *(Chelonia mydas mydas)* **STATUS:** Endangered, overharvested and rapidly vanishing due to high demand for turtle products, i.e., turtle steak and soup. Other causes for the decline include: loss of nesting habitat due to coastal development, fishing lines and nets, boating accidents and artificial beach lighting (which disorient hatchlings away from the sea). A soft-tissue disease called Fibropapilloma threatens the species. Very few hatchlings survive to become adult turtles. **DATA:** Named for the color of their body fat, 28-60" in length, 150-500 pounds. Most gentle of all sea turtles, traced back 150 million years. May take 30 years to mature, maximum lifespan unknown. Some mystery surrounds young turtles spending a "lost year" at sea, going directly into the sea after hatching, and spending their first year at sea, location unknown. They return a year later to shallower waters to mature. Females predictably return to their place of birth. They are believed to have homing instincts and can travel a round trip of approximately 2, 000 miles. **REMARKS:** Complete ban on all turtle products should be strictly enforced. Research of Fibropapilloma should continue. Save-A-Turtle established in the Florida Keys to help the plight of this ancient species.

PAGE 141A
LOWER KEYS MARSH RABBIT *(Sylvilagus palustris hefneri)* **STATUS:** Endangered – approximately 200–400 remain in the wild. Loss of habitat due to development is the primary threat. Also, Feral Cats and road kills threaten the species. **DATA:** Known as "Playboy Bunny" – research was partially financed by the Playboy Corporation. Newly discovered sub-species of Marsh Rabbit (Lazell, 1984). Cranial characteristics separate this sub-species from other Marsh Rabbits. Found exclusively in Lower Keys (Big Pine to Boca Chica), 8-12" in length, dimunitive tail and ears, 2-3 pounds in weight. **DIET:** Native herbs, grasses and plants, fur is darker than its Upper Keys cousin. Essentially nocturnal and shy. **REMARKS:** Near extinction – land acquisitions will be necessary to try to preserve the Lower Keys Marsh Rabbit.

PAGE 141B
BURROWING OWL *(Athene cunicularia)* **STATUS:** Species of special concern. Preferred habitat limited (low vegetation and open fields). Many take refuge at airports and golf courses. Limited genetic diversity due to small and geographically isolated populations. **DATA:** Pigeon-sized, 8" in length, 22" wingspan, short tail, long-legged, with yellow eyes. **DIET:** Small rodents, snakes, lizards and an occasional rabbit. Diurnal (day -active) though most owls are nocturnal. Digs its own hole or burrow in open fields, where it lives and breeds. Both parents tend to the incubation and raising of the young. **REMARKS:** Rare instance where development (of airports and golf courses) has actually helped a species. Comical characters, they will perch near the hole and when approached too closely, will bob up and down, then dive into the hole rather than take flight.

PAGE 164
BROWN PELICAN *(Pelecanus occidentalis)* STATUS: Species of special concern. By 1970's, had almost disappeared from all states which had large population (except Florida). Pesticides in the food chain (Endrin and DDT mainly) resulted in fatally thin-shelled eggs. Following the DDT ban in 1972, pelican started to make a comeback. Still threatened in Florida due to nesting area lost to development, pelicans also are threatened with a slow death sentence if ensnarled in fishing lines. **DATA:** 45 - 54" in length, 90" wingspan, capable of performing spectacular vertical dives in the water pursuing fish (its entire diet). Prominent throat pouch scoops large mouthfuls of seawater and separates out the prey. Nests in colonies in low trees, mangroves or bushes. **REMARKS:** Another species driven to near oblivion because of pesticide poisons. Population now stable, but protection is still necessary. To help a hooked pelican, quietly approach bird, gently grab bill from behind, cut hook barb with wirecutters and pass the rest of the hook back through the skin. Seek professional help for serious injuries.

NOTES:
All species included are found in the Key West area though information reflects all of Florida.

ENDANGERED – In immediate danger of extinction.

THREATENED – Likely to become endangered in near future.

SPECIES OF SPECIAL CONCERN – May become threatened due to human intervention, or has not yet fully recovered from a previous decline (applicable only in Florida).

"What preservation is all about is maintaining a sense of time and place with sensitivity, and linking one's understanding of the past to a consideration for contemporary living."

Sharon L. Wells
Key West historian

KEY WEST ARCHITECTURE

Key West, the last stop at the southern edge of America, exhibits a diverse blend of architectural imprints. For a town that often feels more like part of the Caribbean than the United States, the building stock is impressively grand. Nowhere else in Florida does such a magnificent display of nineteenth century wood frame structures survive. In fact, few other cities can claim such a collection of Victorian and pre-Victorian houses.

These antique dwellings mirror a variety of styles and influences that draw upon a multi-cultural legacy of Bahamian, New England, Creole, Cuban and Victorian influences. Cigarmakers' clapboard cottages, simple and rectangular, sit juxtaposed to ornate mansions once hand-crafted from cypress, pine or mahogany by master builders for successful wreckers, entrepreneurs, spongers and cigar manufacturers.

The size and proportion of the individual frameworks are intrinsic to their value as a collective. A human scale, with one and two-story houses reflective of the early building traditions, and an historic character define the island's built environment.

Key West is a remarkable townscape; one in which texture, light, pattern and rhythm play valuable roles in describing the continually fluid, visual artistry of the architecture on the island-scape. From a well-worn newel post to the simplicity of horizontal pine timbers that create familiar interior rooms — from the intimate scale of neighboring homes to the high, stark symmetry of white pillars that stand out uniquely against the tropical sun — this priceless vernacular architecture is part of America's inheritance, one that must be conserved and protected and appreciated.

Sharon L. Wells

REFERENCES

PAGE 48B
HENRY HASKINS HOUSE
614 Fleming Street
Built: Pre – 1899
Style: Classical Revival
In 1900 this frame residence was home to Egbert P. Ball, publisher of the *Key West Advertiser*. By the Twenties, however, the Henry Haskins family, who was to occupy the home for fifty years, resided here. Haskins, the Assistant Superintendent of the 7th Lighthouse District, died in 1955.
With its second floor windows set high beneath a heavy roof overhang, the splendid Haskins House exemplifies the Eyebrow style, an offshoot of the Classic Revival temple form, and a unique bit of domestic architecture.

PAGE 49
411 WILLIAM STREET
Historic Name: Island City Hotel
Built: 1899 – 1906
Style: Classical Revival
A mammoth renovation project in the Seventies, during which the three-story facade was propped up by telephone poles, gave this old inn a new life. The wraparound porches, double post pillars and roof pediment distinguish this century old monument. Samuel S. Lowe, proprietor of the Island City Hotel when it was one of Key West's first two hotels, charged two dollars a night for guests in 1911.

PAGE 52
ST. PAUL'S EPISCOPAL CHURCH
Duval Street
Style: Gothic Revival
Built: 1914 – 1919
The episcopal church was the pioneer religious organization in Key West. In 1838 a wooden church was erected here and dedicated to St. Paul, the great shipwreck victim. Subsequently, three churches were destroyed by hurricanes or fire. After the 1909 hurricane, architect G.L. Pfeiffer designed this impressive white masonry church in 1914. Bells, inaugurated in 1891 and salvaged from hurricane damage, chime daily. The 8,000 pound organ has 1,100 pipes and was crafted especially for St. Paul's. The 55 beautiful cathedral glass windows, created in Baltimore, are magnificent reflections of a European tradition.

PAGE 53
ST. MARY'S STAR OF THE SEA CHURCH
1010 Windsor Lane
Built: 1905
Builder: Father Anthony Friend
Twin tin-sheathed spires demarcate St. Mary's Star of the Sea from across the island. The first Catholic Church, erected on Duval Street and dedicated in 1852 was destroyed by a fire in the organ reputedly set by an arsonist.
St. Mary's, at the corner of Truman and Windsor, was built at a cost of $30,000 and dedicated on August

20, 1905. It was the only Catholic Church in South Florida. Father Anthony Friend, the first Jesuit priest in Key West, designed the ecclesiastical structure, utilizing stone blocks cut from coral rock dug from the church yard.

PAGES 60,61
1001 EATON STREET
Benito Alfonso / Antonio D. Carrasco House
Built: 1891
Style: Classical Revival

Alfonso, a Cuban-born cigar manufacturer and a patriot to the Cuban revolutionary cause, purchased this lovely Classical Revival gem on January 27, 1891, for $2,000. Several decades later 1001 Eaton became the residence of Antonio Diaz Carrasco, Cuban Consul to Key West from 1903 to 1915. With its encircling verandas, this dwelling was a magnificent setting for Carrasco's official receptions and consulate office. Carrasco, who died in 1915, was buried in the Los Martires de Cuba plot at the Key West Cemetery.

PAGE 70
ERNEST HEMINGWAY HOUSE
907 Whitehead Street
Built: 1851
Style: Spanish Colonial
Builder: Asa F. Tift

Ernest Hemingway's Key West residence, the first home he ever owned, is something of a Moorish-style palace, when compared to the simpler, classic cigarmakers' frame cottages that surround it. Now a National Historic Landmark, the house has a personal history which predates the Civil War.

Owner-builder Asa F. Tift, a wealthy merchant who owned wharves, docks and warehouses on the site of Mallory Square, chose to quarry native coral rock at the site in 1851 for the thick-walled stone mansion and to import Italian marble for the fireplaces.

Pauline Hemingway's uncle paid $8,000 in 1931 for the Tift mansion, which stood, neglected and dilapidated. The residence became the home of the then relatively unknown Ernest and his second wife Pauline. They furnished it with rugs, tiles and furniture from Africa, Cuba and Spain. John Dos Passos, Maxwell Perkins and Sinclair Lewis were among the writers who visited. The spacious, Spanish-Colonial residence features wrought iron rails, palladian windows and the only cellar on the island.

Hemingway's writing studio, perched atop the pool house, and connected to the main house by a catwalk, always was marked by simplicity. The original tile floors, bookcases, hunting trophies, a writing desk and a Royal typewriter are all well preserved today. During the decade of the Thirties, Hemingway's literary career flourished in Key West and his macho image evolved. Already acclaimed for *The Sun Also Rises*, Hemingway penned his masterpieces *To Have and Have Not, Green Hills of Africa* and *For Whom the Bell Tolls* during six-hour writing jags in his studio here.

PAGES 74,75
POST OFFICE / CUSTOM HOUSE
Front Street
Built: 1891
Style: Richardsonian Romanesque
Architect: William Kerr

This magnificent red brick landmark was designed by William Kerr and was completed at a cost of $107,000 in 1891. An imposing 3-1/2 stories, it is the only example, and an unequaled one, of the Richardsonian Romanesque style in south Florida. The ornate decorative terra cotta and brickwork is unsurpassed. Over 918,000 were shipped to Key West for the construction of this government edifice.

The Custom House served as the federal courthouse when Key West was a city of wreckers. In 1898 a U.S. Court of Inquiry convened in a second floor courtroom to investigate the sinking of the USS *Maine* in Havana Harbor, which had sparked the Spanish-American War. Later the Navy Administration was headquartered here. Listed on the National Register of Historic Places in 1973, it will soon reopen, restored to its original grandeur, as a public museum for art and history.

PAGE 80
620 SOUTHARD STREET
John Lowe, Jr. House
Built: 1857 – 1865
Style: Classical Revival
Builder: John Lowe, Jr.

Christmas palms and a coconut grove encircle the proud, pink domicile of John Lowe, Jr., a successful sponge and lumber merchant during the mid-nineteenth century. Lowe operated the town's first sawmill in the 1860's and in 1870 his yacht Magic won the first America's Cup race.

In 1935 Dr. Julius Stone, director of the WPA Emergency Relief Administration, resided here. During the Depression era, Stone was responsible for resurrecting Key West as a tourist mecca in the 1930's.

The grandeur and gardens of the Lowe mansion remains undimmed after nearly a century and a half.

PAGE 81A
313 WILLIAM STREET
George A.T. Roberts House
Built: 1899
Style: Queen Anne

One of the island's masterpieces of Queen Anne styling this elaborate dwelling was erected by George A.T. Roberts. Born in the Bahamas in 1869, Roberts moved to Key West and worked as a cigarmaker for fourteen years. He married Mary Eliza Lowe and became one of the city's most prominent mercantilists, furnishing supplies to sponge fleets in 1900.

The view of Roberts' splendid Victorian mansion, with its turret and double veranda, is most incredible in May when the orange glow of poinciana blooms vividly illuminates the dark charcoal house.

PAGE 81B
615 ELIZABETH STREET
Benjamin P. Baker House
Built: 1892 – 1899
Style: Classical Revival
Builder: Benjamin P. Baker

Often called Key West's "gingerbread house," this elaborate tribute to Victoriana was built by Benjamin P. Baker, an undertaker and embalmer in the 1890's as a wedding gift to his daughter, who married an Illingsworth. The lacy wooden filigree, or gingerbread, are fanciful patterns cut by scroll and jig saws that often lent a touch of individuality and beauty to Conch houses. The local craftsmanship of early ships' carpenters is unmistakable, and still serves as a signature of the skilled woodworkers.

PAGE 81C
811 TRUMAN AVENUE
Newton Curry House
Built: 1911
Style: Classical Revival

Born in Key West in 1879, Newton Curry was the youngest of two sons of Charles Curry and a grandson of William Curry, a Green Turtle Cay native. He was employed as a bookkeeper and cashier for the Key West Ice Company. In 1905 he married Alice Lightbourn, daughter of Walter S. Lightbourn, an owner of the Cortez Cigar Company. For this hip-roofed masonry dwelling, the cement blocks were made on the premises. Together the Currys occupied one of Key West's handsomest residences that lined Truman Avenue, once called Rocky Road and later Division Street.

PAGE 81D
915 DUVAL STREET
Built: Pre – 1912
Style: Classical Revival

A testament to balloon frame construction, 915 Duval Street exhibits a pristine splendor that sets it apart. Painted a glistening white, this stately former residence now houses a well-known restaurant. Two and a half stories and set on limestone piers, this antique Conch house recalls its New England heritage, and still has its original sash windows with opalescent glass panes.

PAGE 84
COAST GUARD BUILDING
Historic Name: Naval Depot and Storehouse
Front Street
Built: 1856 – 1861

The original Naval Depot is the sole surviving building from the earliest naval base on the southernmost island. It was used to store coal for military ships traversing the Atlantic coastal waters during the Civil War.

Constructed of brick, its most singular architectural features are a buttressed pier arcade with 17 arched bays along the north and south elevations and a rooftop cupola. An exterior niche contains a bas relief lighthouse sculpture, referencing the period when the Lighthouse Service was headquartered here. Later occupied by the Coast Guard, the structure is listed on the National Register and was rehabilitated in 1992.

PAGE 85
KEY WEST LIGHTHOUSE MUSEUM
KEY WEST LIGHTHOUSE and KEEPER'S QUARTERS
938 Whitehead Street
Built: 1847

One of the oldest Florida lights, this massive brick lighthouse was erected in 1847 just after the devastating 1846 hurricane. The tower provided the leading light to seven channels for a century. Originally the tower rose 60 feet; in 1894 it was raised another 20 feet. The top of the conical lighthouse, once a prime navigational aid station, now offers a brilliant panoramic view of Old Town.

Coast Guard records document the shipment of a third-order fixed white lens from Paris in 1858. In the earliest days, whale oil was used to power the light. Later power sources include kerosene, incandescent oil vapor, and finally, electricity in 1927. The white clapboard frame Keeper's Quarters was constructed in 1887-88 and restored in 1990. The entire complex houses a museum for exhibits relating to lighthouses, icons of a time past.

PAGE 86A
STRAND THEATER
527 Duval Street
Built: 1934
Builder: Juan Carbonell

This former downtown movie palace built by Juan Carbonell in the Thirties has a fascinating handpainted facade, richly decorated with bowls of fruit, lions and Roman soldiers. The recessed, arched tympanum was restored and the original neon marque refurbished in 1992.

PAGE 86B
LITTLE WHITE HOUSE MUSEUM
Historic Name: Quarters A and B
Address: Front Street
Built: 1890
Style: Frame Vernacular
Architect: George McKay

Erected in 1890 by the U.S. Navy, this double quarters, originally set at the water's edge, housed the naval Paymaster and Commandant. The building was refurbished in 1949 as the winter retreat for President Harry S Truman, who made eleven vacation visits to Key West. Set on an expansive green lawn, the ten room West Indian frame dwelling with jalousied porches became a favorite place for Truman during his presidency. From the house Truman would take a long early walk every morning after a shot of bourbon and a glass of juice. The President and his cronies also made evening poker games on the porch a tradition.

In 1992 this historic structure was carefully restored to re-create its appearance during the Truman era and opened as a presidential museum.

PAGE 87A
1400 DUVAL STREET
J. Vining Harris House
Built: 1900
Style: Queen Anne

Perhaps Key West's most elegant tribute to Queen Anne architecture, the J. Vining Harris House, circa 1900, is a green and pink treasure. Built for a judge and leading political figure, Jeptha Vining Harris, when he married Florida Curry, youngest daughter of William Curry, so-called first millionaire in Florida. The cream colored bricks were shipped from New Orleans.

In the Forties the Harris House opened as a popular waterfront restaurant known as Casa Cayo Hueso, where notables such as Tennessee Williams would bring their guests. It is now a private residence and is still referred to as The Southernmost House.

PAGE 87B
AUDUBON HOUSE
201 Whitehead Street
Built: 1838
Style: West Indian Colonial

The restoration of the dilapidated and almost-condemned Capt. John H. Geiger House in 1958 by Wometco magnate Mitchell Wolfson spearheaded the preservation movement in Key West. The residence had never been altered; indeed, it contained neither running water nor electricity.

Capt. John H. Geiger, a pilot and master wrecker, was the original owner of this corner parcel in the 1830's. According to an early sketch of the city, a large two and a half story residence appears on this site in 1838.

In May, 1832, the great ornithologist John James Audubon visited Captain Geiger in Key West where he discovered the first white-headed pigeon in the United States. The museum exhibits one of the few remaining complete four volume Double Elephant Folios, which includes Audubon's painting of the Key West Pigeon on a bough of geiger flower.

On March 18, 1960, the Wolfson Foundation dedicated the house as a public museum to be named The Audubon House and preserved it as a memorial to the visit by the famed painter to Key West in 1832.

PAGE 125
TRINITY PRESBYTERIAN CHURCH
717 Simonton Street
Built: 1923
Style: Gothic Revival

Erected in 1923 as an English Wesleyan Methodist Church, this prominent edifice originally had a black congregation headed by a white Bahamian pastor. From 1923 to the present, the church has served a Presbyterian congregation. The sun-bleached twin towers flank a gabled front that is highlighted by beautiful stained glass windows.

PAGE 127
KEY WEST CEMETERY
Established 1847

The city cemetery, an extraordinary unique courtyard of tombs and mausoleums, is dead center in Old Town, along Passover and Margaret streets. The 15-acre site dates from 1847 when Windsor Smith deeded a 100-acre tract to the city after the 1846 hurricane had ravaged earlier graveyards. Over the years a Catholic, Jewish and Pauper's cemetery have been added.

A walk through offers intriguing views. Memorabilia graces many tombs—painted roosters, wooden statues, a full-size deer carved from pink granite, photographs inlaid on headstones and the memorable inscription, "I Told You I was Sick." The solitary bronze sailor in the national plot encircled by a silver iron fence, looks over the graveyard and stands amid white marble markers that commemorate the 1898 sinking of the USS Maine.

A visit to the white-on-white above-ground graveyard tells the visitor much about the history, genealogy, Victorian grave art and Key West's ethnic and cultural strands.

PAGE 150
829 EATON STREET
Built: Pre – 1926
Style: Frame Vernacular

Architecturally, this four-square home with a hipped dormer is casual and unpretentious. The window pattern is unusual for Key West, but the tin-shingled roof, which reflects the sun's hot rays and protects against fires, is a defining characteristic of island construction.

PAGE 151
CAPTAIN BENJAMIN SAUNDERS HOUSE
322 Elizabeth Street
Built: 1890
Style: Classical Revival

Capt. Saunders' house, a perfect example of Greek Revivalism in Key West, is a clapboard classic. The porch balustrade gleams. This historic home features high ceilings, hardwood floors and the two-story porches characteristic of the time. The vintage dwelling was built by a wealthy seafarer whose practical carpentry skills were honed aboard schooners. Ashore, the shipbuilders became carpenter-architects, who worked with no formal written plans but relied on practical experience.

PAGE 176
419 SOUTHARD STREET
Built: Pre – 1899
Style: Classical Revival

Typical of the Key West Greek Revival style, this building reflects a hodge podge of changes over time, yet still maintains some original characteristics. The square pilasters, jigcut balusters, double hung windows, double porches, clapboard siding and stringcourses with wooden decorations are time-worn, but distinguishing features.

PAGE 177
724 ASHE STREET
Built: Pre – 1912
Style: Classical Revival

Reminiscent of a scene from *The Rose Tattoo*, filmed in Key West in 1955, this Classic Revival home is an early twentieth century survivor. The collection of ramshackle wooden architecture includes over 2,000 contributing buildings in Key West's Historic District. 724 Ashe, set in a neighborhood of cigar cottages and former cigar factories, is shabby, yet interesting for its flush vertical siding on the building's front.

PAGE 180A
601 CAROLINE STREET
Richard Moore Kemp House
Built: 1887
Style: Classical Revival
Architect: John T. Sawyer

John T. Sawyer, builder of the Armory building, crafted this venerable and graceful Conch house for the Kemp family—spongers and seamen—in 1887, following the Great Fire of 1886. Richard Kemp, an amateur naturalist, identified a previously unknown species of turtle, now called the Kemp turtle.

With its dark, weathered facades, the Kemp Residence stands starkly as one of the island's few unpainted historic structures. Now called the Cypress House, it was constructed with pine timbers. With its long Bahama-style porches, chamfered wood pilasters, and polished patina, it reflects the sense of timelessness that characterizes Key West's built environment.

PAGE 180B
1224 DUVAL STREET
Built: 1892 – 1899
Style: Classical Revival

This handcrafted wooden Conch house displays a singular circular second floor balcony and tapered, round columns which are examples of the electicism that typifies Conch architecture. Well-proportioned with double hung windows that catch the ocean breezes and pink Cuban tile floors on the interior, 1224 Duval is typical of a building style adapted to the tropics and inspired by master carpenters.

PAGE 181
608 ANGELA STREET
Philip Burton House
Built: Pre-1899
Style: Classical Revival

Philip Burton is the world's greatest living Shakespeare scholar. He treasures his privacy and lived in this classically inspired shuttered hideaway beginning in 1974. His restored cross gable cottage, stripped of paint and unblemished by time, is a prize with its zen-like front garden of white rocks and ming aralias.

Born in South Wales, Burton became a prominent director for the BBC, a teacher, playwright and author. Early in his career Burton served as headmaster at the Port Talbot Grammar School where he became the mentor and legal guardian for a young man who was to become the actor Richard Burton.

ACKNOWLEDGEMENTS

I would like to express my gratitude and appreciation to the following individuals for their contributions to this work.

Leslie Artigue, for her creative input, her love, support and inspiration.

Ursula Boll, for her assistance with pre-publication sales, her views, suggestions and friendship.

Steve Hooper, who patiently and methodically guided me through the printing process.

Robert Bender of Creative Services of Key West, for his dedication to perfection in graphic design.

Sheila Sands of Creative Services of Key West and Sharon L Wells for their adept copy editing.

Marty Luko of Solares Hill Design Group, for his creative efforts at the inception of this project.

LT. J.G. Rich Condit, Public Affairs Officer of the U.S. Coast Guard Group Key West
and LT. Robert Klapproth, Commanding Officer of the Coast Guard Cutter "Cushing" for making it
possible for me to observe and photograph an actual rescue at sea of Cuban refugees.

A special thanks to the businesses and organizations that had the faith and foresight to participate in our pre-publication program.

Bayside Inn	Keys Federal Credit Union	Ocean Key House
Chelsea House	Key West Aloe	Old Town Resorts
Conch House	Key West Business Guild	Pier House
First State Bank	Key West Island Book Store	Prudential Knight Realty
The Gardens Hotel	Key West Realty	Reef Relief
Eaton Lodge	La Pensione	Sheraton Suites Key West
Great Southern Group	Little Palm Island	Ted
Hampton Inn Key West	Margaritaville	TIB Bank
Hyatt Key West	Marriott's Casa Marina Resort	Tropical Shell & Gift
Island City House	Marriott's Reach Resort	The Quality Inn

CREDITS

Printing and Binding through Asia Pacific Offset, Inc

Cover Design and Typography – Robert Bender, Creative Services of Key West

Book Design – Alan S. Maltz, assisted by Leslie Artigue

Copy Editing – Sheila Sands, Creative Services of Key West and Sharon L. Wells

TECHNICAL NOTES

The majority of the images included in KEY WEST COLOR were photographed spontaneously.
Fitting the profile of such work is the 35mm format. I use Nikon cameras and lenses, I always have.

The following is a list of equipment and film used to create the images in this book.

Nikon Camera Bodies: F3, F4s, Nikonos IV
Nikon Lenses: 15mm 5.6, Nikonos 15mm 3.5, 55mm 3.5 Macro, 28–85 3.5–4.5 AF Zoom, 80–200 2.8 AF Zoom, 400 3.5 (at times with 1.4x Tele-extender).
Hemingway House (p. 70), *Hemingway Typewriter* (p. 71), and *Key West Sharkatecture* (p. 151), were photographed with a Mamiya RZ and various RZ lens.
Lighting: Either natural or strobe mixed with ambient light; SB24 Speedlight, Vivitar 285.
Macro flower images included in the Introduction were photographed with a Unitron Ringlight and ambient light.
Film: Fujichrome Velvia, Fujichrome 50, Kodachrome 25.

Any questions pertaining to technique or style may be directed to the publisher.